SEAGRASS DREAMS

A COUNTING BOOK

Kathleen M. Hanes

Illustrations by
Chloe Bonfield

Seagrass Press
Lake Forest, California

SEA
GRASS

SEAGRASS

IN THE SHALLOW PARTS OF OCEANS all around the globe, one can find seagrass rooted to the seafloor. These plants take many different forms. The *blades* of some species are long, flat strips, while others grow as narrow, hollow tubes. Often, several species of seagrass are found growing mixed with one another, in vast meadows.

Seagrass blades, swaying back and forth with the water currents and waves, create a hypnotizing landscape that is as useful as it is beautiful. These meadows help prevent soil erosion and store an enormous amount of carbon that prevents the ocean from becoming too acidic.

Seagrass also provides an important habitat in which marine animals can safely reproduce. They are a calm haven for juveniles of numerous species, since the dense blades allow the young to hide, safe from predators, while they grow.

The rich diversity of organisms in *seagrass meadows* offers a wide variety of food for all the animals that live there.

1 **ONE** great barracuda floats over the seagrass meadow, scales flashing. His jaws open and close slowly, as he watches for the small fish that will be his dinner.

TWO yellow stingrays lie partly buried in the sand beneath the seagrass blades, searching for small *shrimp* and *worms* to eat. The rays stay hidden from sight until they wriggle a fin.

2

3

THREE young queen conchs, protected by their flared *shells*, creep slowly along. They scrape up *algae* and dead seagrass blades with their rough tongues.

FOUR dugongs, two mothers and their calves, roam. They rip up seagrass by the roots with their wide, flat *muzzles*, gobbling down the blades and leaving a trail of muddy sand in their wake.

FIVE tubular sea cucumbers ooze their way through the seagrass blades, vacuuming up tiny plants and animals from the sand. When threatened, the cucumbers discharge some of their *internal organs* to scare off predators.

SIX bucktooth parrotfish dart from one *clump* of seagrass to another, changing their colors and patterns to stay *camouflaged*. These fish skim over the meadow, pecking at the fuzzy algae coating the blades.

SEVEN chocolate chip sea stars gather together to attack soft *corals* and *sponges*. They eject bright orange stomachs out of their mouths to smother and digest *prey*.

EIGHT Long Island bay scallops cling to seagrass blades, holding on by tiny threads. The scallops perch safely, swaying high above the *lobsters* and *snails* that want to eat them.

8

NINE California spiny lobsters assemble in a clump, tiptoeing through the meadow of seagrass. They find and crack shells, nibbling on the scallops and *mussels* inside.

9

TEN collector urchins cruise across the ocean floor, hungrily stuffing seagrass pieces into their tiny mouths. Torn blades float in their wake.

10

SOME FUN FACTS

1 GREAT BARRACUDA

(Sphyraena barracuda)

The barracuda feeds on smaller fish and is an ambush predator, relying on stealth and great bursts of speed (up to 35 miles/56 kilometers per hour) to surprise its prey.

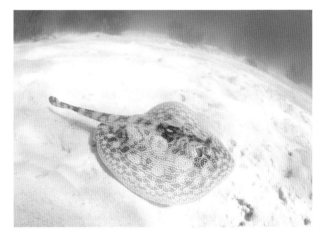

2 YELLOW STINGRAY

(Urobatis jamaicensis)

The mouths of these stingrays are located on the underside of their bodies. They have strong jaws to crack open the shells of the *mollusks* they eat. Like the barracuda, they also rely on ambush to catch their prey.

3 QUEEN CONCH

(Lobatus gigas)

Conch shells can be used for money, jewelry, or even musical instruments. The animals themselves are often eaten and can be prepared as cracked conch, conch fritters, or conch stew.

4 DUGONG

(Dugong dugon)

Dugongs are distantly related to elephants, although they don't look or act much like them. Dugongs can hold their breath underwater for up to six minutes at a time. Babies stay with their mothers for the first 18 months of life.

5 TUBULAR SEA CUCUMBER

(Holothuria tubulosa)

This sea cucumber has tough, leathery skin and can grow up to 12 inches/30 centimeters long. It covers itself with a protective layer of mucus, but is still hunted by divers for food in many Asian countries.

6 BUCKTOOTH PARROTFISH

(Sparisoma radians)

This fish, a very common algae eater on Caribbean coral reefs, is one of the smallest and least colorful in the parrotfish family. Some bucktooth parrotfish begin life as males, but most begin as females and become males later on.

7 CHOCOLATE CHIP SEA STAR

(Protoreaster nodosus)

This sea star, like its relatives the sea cucumber and sea urchin, uses its tube feet to move across the ocean floor. The tube feet are filled with water and feel squishy. Each sea star has thousands of them to move the animal along.

8 LONG ISLAND BAY SCALLOP

(Argopecten irradians)

When not attached to seagrass blades, these scallops move quickly through the water by "clapping" their shells (also called valves) together, forcing water out behind them. Their 18 pairs of eyes detect shadows and movement around them.

9 CALIFORNIA SPINY LOBSTER

(Panulirus interruptus)

Though this lobster does not have claws, it can defend itself by making a loud noise. The lobster is almost entirely nocturnal, meaning it is active at night. Juveniles usually hide in dense seagrass to protect themselves.

10 COLLECTOR URCHIN

(Tripneustes gratilla)

This sea urchin has five sharp teeth in its mouth on the underside of its body as well as venomous spines to protect itself. Its name refers to the bits of algae and strips of seaweed and seagrass it collects all over its back, probably to camouflage itself.

GLOSSARY

ALGAE – plant-like organisms that live in water or damp areas and lack flowers, true roots, stems, and leaves

BLADE – the broad part of a plant leaf

CAMOUFLAGE – the hiding or disguising of a plant or animal to prevent it from being seen

CLUMP – a group of organisms that are very close together

CORAL – a small marine animal that usually lives in colonies and often forms a stony skeleton around itself for protection

INTERNAL ORGAN – a part of an animal that is inside its body and performs a certain job

LOBSTER – a large marine crustacean with a long abdomen and five pairs of walking legs

MOLLUSK – an animal without a backbone, with a soft body that is usually protected by a hard shell

MUSSEL – a mollusk with paired shells, living in either salt water or freshwater

MUZZLE –part of the face of an animal, containing the nose and mouth, that sticks out

PREY – any animal eaten by another animal for food

SEAGRASS MEADOW – a large area of seagrass that looks like a grassland or prairie

SHELL – a hard, protective, outer case

SHRIMP – a small crustacean with a long abdomen that is free-swimming and usually lives in the ocean

SNAIL – a mollusk with a single, spiral shell

SPONGE – an animal without a backbone that stays attached to the ocean floor and sucks water through its body, filtering out microscopic organisms

WORM – an animal without a backbone that lacks limbs

LOCATIONS OF SEAGRASS MEADOWS AROUND THE WORLD

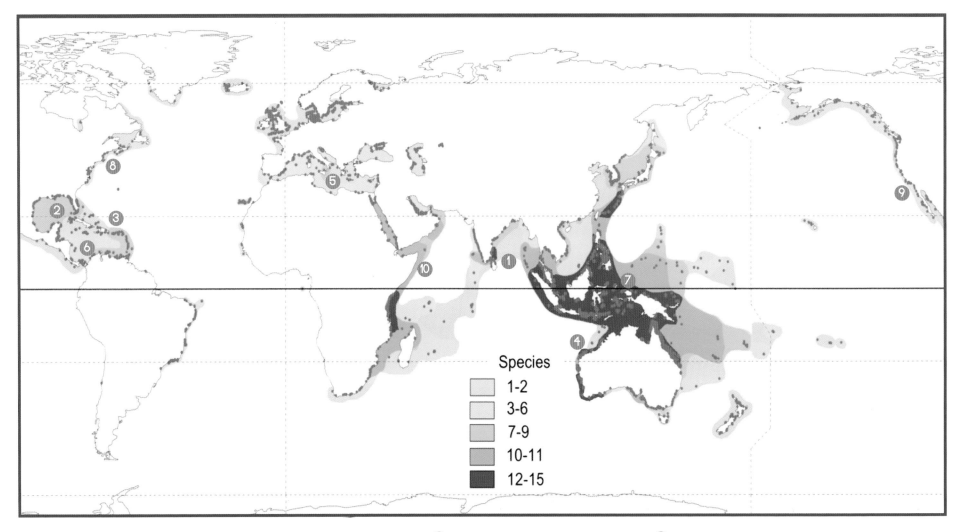

Species
- 1-2
- 3-6
- 7-9
- 10-11
- 12-15

Seagrass grows in shallow, coastal areas of oceans around the world. More species tend to be found in warm waters near the equator. Each number on the map shows an area where each animal in this book can be found.

① Great Barracuda
② Yellow Stingrays
③ Queen Conchs
④ Dugongs
⑤ Tubular Sea Cucumbers
⑥ Bucktooth Parrotfish
⑦ Chocolate Chip Sea Stars
⑧ Long Island Bay Scallops
⑨ California Spiny Lobsters
⑩ Collector Urchins

THE WORLD SEAGRASS ASSOCIATION (WSA) published a statement in 2016 after its 12th International Seagrass Biology Workshop calling for both governmental and non-governmental agencies around the world to take stronger actions to ensure the continued health of seagrass meadows. If you are interested in learning more about the work being done by the WSA, please visit: http://wsa.seagrassonline.org/securing-a-future-for-seagrass.

REFERENCES

Florida Department of Environmental Protection

www.dep.state.fl.us/coastal/habitats/seagrass

Florida Fish and Wildlife Conservation Commission

http://myfwc.com/research/habitat/seagrasses/information/importance

Florida Keys National Marine Sanctuary

http://floridakeys.noaa.gov/plants/seagrass.html

Global Seagrass Monitoring Network

www.seagrassnet.org

International Union for the Conservation of Nature

www.iucn.org/content/seagrass-habitat-declining-globally

National Center for Ecological Analysis and Synthesis

http://kids.nceas.ucsb.edu/biomes/seagrass%20fact%20sheet-1.pdf

National Geographic Ocean Views

http://voices.nationalgeographic.com/2014/03/31/whatsanacreofseagrassworth

Project Seagrass

www.projectseagrass.org

Seagrass Watch

www.seagrasswatch.org/seagrass.html

Smithsonian Institution Ocean Portal

http://ocean.si.edu/seagrass-and-seagrass-beds

World Seagrass Association

http://wsa.seagrassonline.org

To my mother,
who has always believed in the translocation
of nutrients along seagrass rhizomes. — K.M.H.

To Charlotte,
for sharing the wonder of
the world with me. — C.B.

Quarto is the authority on a wide range of topics. Quarto
educates, entertains, and enriches the lives of our
readers—enthusiasts and lovers of hands-on living.
www.quartoknows.com

Words in italics within the text can be found in the glossary toward the end of the book.

Design: Nick Tiemersma

Library of Congress Cataloging-in-Publication Data has been applied for.

6 Orchard Road, Suite 100
Lake Forest, CA 92630
quartoknows.com
Visit our blogs at quartoknows.com

Printed in China
1 3 5 7 9 10 8 6 4 2

MIX
Paper from
responsible sources
FSC® C101537